'BAIL MATTERS', SUPREME COURT'S LATEST LEADING CASE LAWS

CASE NOTES- FACTS- FINDINGS OF APEX COURT JUDGES & CITATIONS

JAYPRAKASH BANSILAL SOMANI
ADVOCATE SUPREME COURT OF INDIA

Copyright © Jayprakash Bansilal Somani Advocate Supreme Court Of India
All Rights Reserved.

ISBN 978-1-68563-191-8

This book has been published with all efforts taken to make the material error-free after the consent of the author. However, the author and the publisher do not assume and hereby disclaim any liability to any party for any loss, damage, or disruption caused by errors or omissions, whether such errors or omissions result from negligence, accident, or any other cause.

While every effort has been made to avoid any mistake or omission, this publication is being sold on the condition and understanding that neither the author nor the publishers or printers would be liable in any manner to any person by reason of any mistake or omission in this publication or for any action taken or omitted to be taken or advice rendered or accepted on the basis of this work. For any defect in printing or binding the publishers will be liable only to replace the defective copy by another copy of this work then available.

Dedicated

To

All the Past & Present Judges of the Supreme Court of India.

Salute to their wisdom.

Salute to their interpretation of Law.

Salute to their elaborative judgement writing.

Contents

Preface — vii
Acknowledgements — ix

1. Sushila Aggarwal Vs State (nct Of Delhi), 2020 — 1
2. Arnab Manoranjan Goswami Vs.the State Of Maharashtra And Ors., 2020 — 6
3. Bikramjit Singh Vs. The State Of Punjab, 2020 — 9
4. Jatinderveer Arora And Ors Vs. State Of Punjab, 2020 — 11
5. National Alliance For People's Movements And Ors. Vs. The State Of Maharashtra And Ors., 2020 — 13
6. P. Chidambaram Vs. Directorate Of Enforcement, 2019 — 16
7. Prathvi Raj Chauhan Vs. Union Of India (uoi) And Ors. 2020 — 19
8. Saravanan Vs. State Represented By The Inspector Of Police, 2020 — 22
9. Sumetivij Vs. Paramount Tech Fab Industries, 2021 — 25
10. The State Of Kerala Vs. Mahesh, 2021 — 27
11. Aparna Bhat And Ors Vs State Of Madhya Pradesh, 2021 — 29
12. Girraj Vs Kiranpal And Ors,2021 — 32
13. Kanakarajan Vs State Of Kerala, 2017 — 34
14. Naveen Singh Vs The State Of Uttar Pradesh, 2021 — 36
15. Union Of India Vs Prateek Shukla, 2021 — 39
16. Union Of India (uoi) Vs. K.a. Najeeb, 2020 — 41
17. Naresh Kumar Mangla Vs. Anita Agarwal And Ors., 2020 — 44
18. Venkatesan Balasubramaniyan And Ors.vs. The Intelligence Officer, D.r.i. Bangalore, 2020 — 47
19. R. Damodaran Vs. The State Represented By The Inspector Of Police, 2021 — 49
20. 20. Mauji Ram Vs. State Of Uttar Pradesh And Ors, 2019 — 51

Videos & Tv Shows On Law & Exim — 53

Contents

List Of Books 59

Preface

Dear Learned Advocates of Trial Courts, High Courts & Supreme Court,

I am very delighted to provide you a book on 'Bail Matters - Supreme Court of India's Latest Leading Case Laws'.

In this book you will get...

1. Name of the Case i. e. Cause title
2. Relevant Sections discussed in the case
3. Hon'ble Judges/Coram of the case
4. Number of PDF Pages in Original Judgement of the case
5. All available Citations of the case
6. Case Note with appeal allowed/ dismissed or disposed off
7. Facts of the case
8. Hon'ble Apex Court's findings, while dismissing/allowing or disposing the appeal
9. Ratio Decidendi if any.

My special thanks to Manupatra, because of their web portal I can compile this book in well manner. I am also thankful to Notion Press to support me to publish & market this book throughout the Country. Thanks to my Juniors, Advocate Colleagues & Insolvency Professional Colleagues to support me in this venture.

Miss Simran Mehta has helped me a lot in the compilation of this book.

I hope this book will add some value addition in the wealth of your legal knowledge. Your positive feedbacks will boost me to compile/ write further books & negative feedbacks will improve my skills. Kindly send your valuable feedbacks by email.

Yours Sincerely,
Jayprakash B. Somani
Advocate, Supreme Court of India
Email: jaysomani64@gmail.com
Web Site: www.jayprakashsomani.com
Call: 8384051134, 9322188701

Acknowledgements

Printed & Published by
Notion Press
No. 8, 3rdCross Street,
CIT Colony, Mylapore,
Chennai, Tamil Nadu- 600004

• • •

Managed by
Jayprakash Somani Advocates & Solicitors
Law Firm for Supreme Court of India
Delhi Office
257 C, Pocket 1, Mayur Vihar Phase 1, Delhi 110091.
Call 8384051134, 9322188701, 8459194576, 01141051516
Supreme Court Chamber
312, 3rd Floor, M. C. Setalvad Block, In front of 'D' Gate, Bhagwan Das Road, Supreme Court of India, New Delhi 110001
Contact: 8459194576, 9811011747
www.jayprakashsomani.com

• • •

Books are available online at
1. **Notion Press:**https://notionpress.com/author/jayprakash_somani
2. **Amazon:**https://www.amazon.in/s?k=jayprakash+somani
3. **Flipkart:**https://www.flipkart.com/search?q=Jayprakash%20Somani

• • •

CHAPTER I

Sushila Aggarwal Vs State (NCT Of Delhi), 2020

Relevant Sections:

- CRPC- Sections 167(2),437(2),437(3), 438, 438(1), 438(2) and 439(2)

Hon'ble judges: Arun Mishra, Indira Banerjee, Vineet Saran, M.R. Shah and S. Ravindra Bhat, JJ.

No. of pdf pages in Original Judgment: 78

Equivalent Citations: 2020(209)AIC129, AIR2020SC831, 2020ALLMR(Cri)497, 2020 (111) ACC 528, 2020(2)ACR1907, 2020(2)ADJ322, 2020(8)ADJ389, 2020(2)BLJ186, 2020(2)BomCR(Cri)1, 2020(1)Crimes225(SC), 2020CriLJ1590, 266(2020)DLT741, 2020GLH(2)265, (2020)3GLR2303, ILR2020(1)Kerala517, 2020(2)JLJ431, 2020(1)J.L.J.R.480, 2020(1)JKJ333[SC], 2020 (1) KHC 663, 2020(1)KLT545, 2020-2-LW(Crl)161, MANU/SC/0100/2020, 2020(1)PLJR524, 2020(1)RLW373(SC), 2020(1)RCR(Criminal)833

Overruled/Reversed:
SiddharamSatlingappaMhetre v. State of Maharashtra and Ors.;
SalauddinAbdulsamad Shaikh v. State of Maharashtra;
K.L. Verma v. State and Anr.;
Sunita Devi v. State of Bihar and Anr.;
Nirmal Jeet Kaur v. State of M.P.;
HDFC Bank Ltd. v. J.J. Mannan @ J.M. John Paul and Anr.;
Adri Dharan Das v. State of West Bengal;
Naresh Kumar Yadav v. Ravindra Kumar and Ors.;
Satpal Singh v. State of Punjab

Case note: Criminal - Anticipatory bail - Determination of duration - Sections 167(2), 437(2),437(3), 438, 438(1), 438(2) and 439(2) of Code of Criminal Procedure, 1973 - Present reference filed to determine duration of protection granted to person under Section 438 of Code should be limited to fixed period so as to enable person to surrender before Trial Court and seek regular bail - Whether anticipatory bail under Section 438 of Code should be limited to fixed period so as to enable person to surrender before Trial Court and seek regular bail and life of anticipatory bail should end at time and stage when Accused was summoned by court.

Facts: In the light of the conflicting views of the different Benches of varying strength, the present reference had been filed to determine duration of protection granted to person under Section 438 of Code should be limited to fixed period so as to enable the person to surrender before Trial Court and seek regular bail.

Held, while answering the reference:

M.R. Shah, J.

(i) The decision of the Constitution Bench in the case of Gurbaksh Singh Sibbia holds the field for number of years and the same has been followed by all the Courts in the country. While granting anticipatory bail, normally conditions were imposed by the court/courts which as such are in consonance with the decision of the Constitution Bench in the case of Gurbaksh Singh Sibbia and Section 438(2) read with Section 437(3) of the Code of Criminal Procedure. If breach of any of the above conditions is committed, the order of anticipatory bail would be cancelled. It would be open to the Investigating Officer to file an application for remand, and the concerned Magistrate would decide it on merits, without influenced by the grant of anticipatory bail order. However, in the case of Siddharam Satlingappa Mhetre, despite the specific observations by the Constitution Bench of this Court in Gurbaksh Singh Sibbia that the normal Rule should be not to limit the operation of the order in relation to a period of time, in other words in an appropriate case and looking to the facts and circumstances of the case and the stage at which the pre-arrest bail application was made, the court concerned can limit the operation of the order in relation to a period of time, on absolute misreading of the judgment in the case of Gurbaksh Singh Sibbia and just contrary to the observations made, an absolute proposition of law was laid down that the life of the order under Section 438, Code of Criminal Procedure granting bail cannot be curtailed. Despite the clear cut observations made by the Constitution Bench in Gurbaksh Singh Sibbia, in the case of Salauddin Abdulsamad Shaikh, this Court had observed and held that the order of anticipatory bail has to be necessarily limit in time frame. In many cases subsequently the decision in the case of Salauddin Abdulsamad Shaikh had been followed, despite the specific observations made by the Constitution Bench in Gurbaksh Singh Sibbia which, as such, were just contrary to the view taken in subsequent decisions in the cases of Siddharam Satlingappa Mhetre and Salauddin Abdulsamad Shaikh. At this stage, it was required to be noted that in the case of Salauddin Abdulsamad Shaikh, this Court had not at all considered the decision of the Constitution Bench in the case of Gurbaksh Singh Sibbia. It could not be disputed that the decision of this Court in the case of Gurbaksh Singh Sibbia was a Constitution Bench decision which was binding unless it was upset by a larger Bench than the Constitution Bench. Therefore, considering the decision of the Constitution Bench of this Court in the case of Gurbaksh Singh Sibbia and the relevant observations, the decision of this Court in the case of Siddharam Satlingappa Mhetre to the extent it takes the view that the life of the order under Section 438 Code of Criminal Procedure cannot be curtailed was not a correct law in light of the observations made by the Constitution Bench in Gurbaksh Singh Sibbia. The decision of this Court in the case of Salauddin Abdulsamad Shaikh which takes an extreme view that the order of anticipatory bail had to be necessarily limited in time frame was also not a good law and is against and just contrary to the decision of this Court in the case of Gurbaksh Singh Sibbia, which was a Constitution Bench judgment. [7.4]

(ii) Thus, considering the observations made by the Constitution Bench of this Court in the case of Gurbaksh Singh Sibbia, the court may, if there are reasons for doing so, limit the operation of the order to a short period only after filing of an FIR in respect of the matter covered by order and the applicant may in such case be directed to obtain an order of bail under Sections 437 or 439 of the Code within a reasonable short period after the filing of the FIR. The Constitution Bench had further observed that the same need not be followed as an invariable rule. It was further observed and held that normal Rule should be not to limit the operation of the order in relation to a period of time. The conditions could be imposed by the concerned court while granting pre-arrest bail order including limiting the operation of the order in relation to a period of time if the circumstances so warrant, more particularly the stage at which the anticipatory bail application was moved, namely, whether the same was at the stage before the FIR was filed or at the stage when the FIR was filed and the investigation was in progress or at the stage when the investigation was complete and the charge sheet was filed. However, the normal Rule should be not to limit the order in relation to a period of time. [7.5]

S. Ravindra Bhat, J.

(i) Where the Parliament wished to exclude or restrict the power of courts, under Section 438 of the Code, it did so in categorical terms. Parliament's omission to restrict the right of citizens, Accused of other offences from the right to seek anticipatory bail, necessarily leads one to assume that neither a blanket restriction can be read into by this Court, nor can inflexible guidelines in the exercise of discretion, be insisted upon-that would amount to judicial legislation. [63]

(ii) There was no offence, per se, which stands excluded from the purview of Section 438, - except the offences mentioned in Section 438(4). In other words, anticipatory bail could be granted, having regard to all the circumstances, in respect of all offences. At the same time, if there were indications in any special law or statute, which exclude relief under Section 438(1) they would have to be duly considered. Also, whether anticipatory offences should be granted, in the given facts and circumstances of any case, where the allegations relating to the commission of offences of a serious nature, with certain special conditions, was a matter of discretion to be exercised, having regard to the nature of the offences, the facts shown, the background of the applicant, the likelihood of his fleeing justice, likelihood of co-operation or non-co-operation with the investigating agency or police, etc. There could be no inflexible time frame for which an order of anticipatory bail can continue. [75]

(iii) It was held in Gursharan Singh that the release by grant of bail of an Accused under Section 167(2) amounts to deemed bail. This was borne out by Section 167(2) which states that anyone released on bail under its provision shall be deemed to be so released under the provisions of Chapter XXXIII for the purposes of that Chapter. The judgment in Aslam Babalal Desai had clarified that when an Accused is released by operation of Section 167(2) and subsequently, a charge-sheet is filed, there is no question of the cancellation of his bail. In these circumstances, the mere fact that an Accused was given relief under Section 438 at one stage, per se did not mean that upon the filing of a charge-sheet, he is necessarily to surrender or/and apply for regular bail. The analogy to deemed bail under Section 167(2) with anticipatory bail leads this Court to conclude that the mere subsequent event of the filing of a charge-sheet could not compel the Accused to surrender and seek regular bail. As a matter of fact, interestingly, if indeed, if a charge-sheet was filed where the Accused is on anticipatory bail, the normal implication would be that there was no occasion for the investigating agency or the police to require his custody, because there would have been nothing in his behavior requiring such a step. In other words, an Accused, who was granted anticipatory bail would continue to be at liberty when the charge sheet was filed, the natural implication is that there is no occasion for a direction by the Court that he be arrested and further that he had cooperated with the investigation. At the same time, however, at any time during the investigation were any occasion to arise calling for intervention of the court for infraction of any of the conditions imposed under Section 437(3) read with Section 438(2) or the violation of any other condition imposed in the given facts of a case, recourse can always be had under Section 439(2). [77]

(iv) Therefore, it was held that the protection granted under Section 438 Code of Criminal Procedure should not always or ordinarily be limited to a fixed period, it should inure in favour of the Accused without any restriction as to time. Usual or standard conditions under Section 437(3) read with Section 438(2) should be imposed if there were peculiar features in regard to any crime or offence (such as seriousness or gravity etc.), it was open to the court to impose any appropriate condition (including fixed nature of relief, or its being tied to an event or time bound) etc. The life of an anticipatory bail did not end generally at the time and stage when the Accused was summoned by the court, or after framing charges, but could also continue till the end of the trial. However, if there were any special or peculiar features necessitating the court to limit the tenure of anticipatory bail, it was open for it to do so. [84]

∙ ∙ ∙

CHAPTER II

Arnab Manoranjan Goswami Vs.The State of Maharashtra and Ors., 2020

Relevant Sections:

- IPC- s. 306, 34
- CRPC- s. 482, 439

Hon'ble judges: Dr. D.Y. Chandrachud and Indira Banerjee, JJ.
No. of pdf pages in Original Judgment: 33
Equivalent Citations: AIR2021SC1, 2020ALLMR(Cri)4347, 2021 (1) ALT (Crl.) 1 (A.P.), 2020(4)Crimes428(SC), 2021CriLJ517, 2021(1)JLJ102, 2021(1)J.L.J.R.169, 2020(4)MLJ(Crl)639, MANU/SC/0902/2020, 2021(I)OLR13, 2021(1)PLJR85, 2021(1)RLW179(SC), (2021)2SCC427

Case note: Criminal - Quashing - First Information Report (FIR) and Arrest memo - Section 482 of the Code of Criminal Procedure, 1973 (CrPC) - Illegal arrest - Wrongful detention - Interim Relief - Release from custody and a stay of proceedings including investigation in pursuance of the FIR - Division Bench declined to accede to the prayer for the grant of bail - High Court held that since the Appellant was in judicial custody, it was open to him to avail of the remedy of bail Under Section 439 of the CrPC - Appellant aggrieved by the denial of his interim prayer for the grant of bail in present appeal - Whether Appellant entitled to interim relief as sought in form of grant of bail?

Facts: The Appellant, Editor-in-Chief of an English television news channel, Republic TV was arrested on 4 November 2020 in connection with FIR registered under Sections 306 and 34 of the Indian Penal Code. The genesis of the FIR could be traced back to December 2016, when a company by the name of ARG Outlier Media Private Limited (ARG) awarded a contract for civil and interior work to another company, Concorde Design Private Limited (CDPL) which was owned substantially by one AnvayNaik (the deceased). Spouse of the deceased alleged to have committed suicide. The contents of the FIR included Appellant for abating death of deceased and his spouse due to non-payment of their legitimate dues. Appellant claimed arrest to have been vitiated by malice in fact. Appellant submitted that his arrest is rooted in malice which is evident from the manner in which he was targeted for his news broadcasts criticizing the Maharashtra government and the Maharashtra police. It was further claimed that following the acceptance of police report and reinvestigation ordered at the behest of the Home Minister of the State of Maharashtra as ultra vires and in the absence of the specific permission of the CJM, it was not open to the State to conduct a reinvestigation; It was further contended that FIR in question did not establish an offence under Section 306 read with Section 34 of the Indian Penal Code.

Hon'ble Apex Court held, while disposing the appeal:

High Court in the present case misdirected itself in declining to enquire prima facie on a petition for quashing whether the parameters in the exercise of that jurisdiction have been duly established and if so whether a case for the grant of interim bail has been made out. The settled principles which have been consistently reiterated since the judgment of this Court in the case of State of Haryana v. BhajanLal include a situation where the allegations made in the FIR or the complaint, even if they are taken at their face value and accepted in their entirety, do not prima facie constitute any offence or make out a case against the Accused.

The High Court recited the legal position that the jurisdiction to quash under Section 482 has to be exercised sparingly. These words, however, are not meaningless incantations, but have to be assessed with reference to the contents of the particular FIR before the High Court. If the High Court were to carry out a prima facie evaluation, it would have been impossible for it not to notice the disconnect between the FIR and the provisions of Section 306 of the Indian Penal Code. The failure of the High Court to do so has led it to adopting a position where it left the Appellant to pursue his remedies for regular bail under Section 439. The High Court was clearly in error in failing to perform a duty which is entrusted to it while evaluating a petition under Section 482 albeit at the interim stage.

The petition before the High Court was instituted Under Article 226 of the Constitution and Section 482 of the Code of Criminal Procedure. While dealing with the petition under Section 482 for quashing the FIR, the High Court has not considered whether prima facie the ingredients of the offence have been made out in the FIR. If the High Court were to have carried out this exercise, it would have been apparent that the ingredients of the offence have not prima facie been established. As a consequence of its failure to perform its function under Section 482, the High Court has disabled itself from exercising its jurisdiction under Article 226 to consider the Appellant's application for bail. In considering such an application under Article 226, the High Court must be circumspect in exercising its powers on the basis of the facts of each case. However, the High Court should not foreclose itself from the exercise of the power when a citizen has been arbitrarily deprived of their personal liberty in an excess of state power.

While considering an application for the grant of bail under Article 226 in a suitable case, the High Court must consider the settled factors namely,(i) The nature of the alleged offence, the nature of the accusation and the severity of the punishment in the case of a conviction;(ii) Whether there exists a reasonable apprehension of the Accused tampering with the witnesses or being a threat to the complainant or the witnesses;(iii) The possibility of securing the presence of the Accused at the trial or the likelihood of the Accused fleeing from justice;(iv) The antecedents of and circumstances which are peculiar to the Accused;(v) Whether prima facie the ingredients of the offence are made out, on the basis of the allegations as they stand, in the FIR; and(vi) The significant interests of the public or the State and other similar considerations.

Since the proceedings are pending before the High Court, the observations on the facts contained in the present judgment confined to a determination whether a case for grant of interim protection was made out.

The interim protection granted by the order dated 11 November 2020 shall continue to remain in operation pending the disposal of the proceedings before the High Court and as directed.

Ratio Decidendi:

High Court must exercise its power with caution and circumspection, cognizant of the fact that its jurisdiction is not a ready substitute for recourse to the remedy of bail under Section 439 of the Code of Criminal Procedure.

• • •

CHAPTER III

Bikramjit Singh vs. The State of Punjab, 2020

Relevant Sections: IPC- s.302, 307, 452, 427, 341, 34 CRPC- s.167(2)
Hon'ble Judges: *Rohinton Fali Nariman, Navin Sinha and K.M. Joseph, JJ.*
No. of pdf pages in Original Judgment: 28
Equivalent Citations:2020(215)AIC104, 2020 (3) ALT (Crl.) 281 (A.P.), 2021(1)BLJ118, 2020(4)Crimes339(SC), 2021(1)JLJ62, 2020(4)J.L.J.R.240, 2020(5)JKJ194[SC], 2020(4)MLJ(Crl)376, MANU/SC/0749/2020, 2020(4)PLJR263, 2020(4)RLW3056(SC), (2020)10SCC616

Case note: Criminal - Default Bail -Section 167(2) of the Code of Criminal Procedure, 1963 (CrPC) - First Information Report (FIR) registered against Appellant - Sections 302, 307, 452, 427, 341, 34 of the Indian Penal Code, 1860 read with Section 25 of the Arms Act, 1959, Sections 3, 4, 5, 6 of the Explosive Substances Act, 1908 and Section 13 of the Unlawful Activities (Prevention) Act, 1967 (UAPA)- No chargesheet filed after 90 days of custody - Application seeking default bail dismissed by Magistrate on the ground that 90 days' time being extended to 180 days - Special Court in appeal set aside the order for want of jurisdiction - High Court vide impugned judgment confirmed powers of Magistrate to extend the time - It was held that in case investigation is done by State police, the Magistrate empowered to extend the period of investigation upto 180 days - Hence, the present appeal.

Facts: The present case pertains to claim of default which was denied to the Appellant. The appellant was apprehended in FIR registered under Sections 302, 307, 452, 427, 341, 34 of the Indian Penal Code, 1860 read with Section 25 of the Arms Act, 1959, Sections 3, 4, 5, 6 of the Explosive Substances Act, 1908 and Section 13 of the Unlawful Activities (Prevention) Act, 1967 (UAPA). Appellant remained in custody and no charge sheet was filed within 90 days, as stipulated in law. Appellant moved default bail application which was rejected by Sub-Divisional Magistrate on the ground of time being extended to 180 days. An appeal was preferred before the Special Court which set aside the order on the ground that any extension of time could be granted by it and not the Court of Sub Divisional Magistrate for want of jurisdiction. High Court however reversed the finding on the ground that Magistrate is empowered to extend the time in the circumstances of present case as investigation was being conducted by State Police and therefore case can be committed to Sessions Court. Hence, the present appeal.

Hon'ble Apex Court held, while dismissing the appeal: A conspectus of the aforesaid decisions would show that so long as an application for grant of default bail is made on expiry of the period of 90 days (which application need not even be in writing) before a charge sheet is filed, the right to default bail becomes complete. It is of no moment that the Criminal Court in question either does not dispose of such application before the charge sheet is filed or disposes of such application wrongly before such charge sheet is filed. So long as an application has been made for default bail on expiry of the stated period before time is further extended to the maximum period of 180 days, default bail, being an indefeasible right of the Accused under the first proviso to Section 167(2), kicks in and must be granted.

High Court wholly incorrect in stating that once the challan was presented by the prosecution on 25.03.2019 as an application was filed by the Appellant on 26.03.2019, the Appellant is not entitled to default bail. First and foremost, the High Court has got the dates all wrong. The application that was made for default bail was made on or before 25.02.2019 and not 26.03.2019. The charge sheet was filed on 26.03.2019 and not 25.03.2019. The fact that this application was wrongly dismissed on 25.02.2019 would make no difference and ought to have been corrected in revision. The sole ground for dismissing the application was that the time of 90 days had already been extended by the learned Sub-Divisional Judicial Magistrate, Ajnala by his order dated 13.02.2019. This Order was correctly set aside by the Special Court by its judgment dated 25.03.2019, holding that under the UAPA read with the NIA Act, the Special Court alone had jurisdiction to extend time to 180 days under the first proviso in Section 43-D(2)(b). The fact that the Appellant filed yet another application for default bail on 08.04.2019, would not mean that this application would wipe out the effect of the earlier application that had been wrongly decided. The right to default bailare not mere statutory rights under the first proviso to Section 167(2) of the Code, but is part of the procedure established by law Under Article 21 of the Constitution of India, which is, therefore, a fundamental right granted to an Accused person to be released on bail once the conditions of the first proviso to Section 167(2) are fulfilled.

• • •

CHAPTER IV

Jatinderveer Arora and Ors vs. State of Punjab, 2020

Relevant Sections: CRPC- s.406
  Hon'ble judges:_Hrishikesh Roy, J._
  No. of pdf pages in Original Judgment: 7
  Equivalent Citations:2021(217)AIC177, AIR2021SC760, 2020(4)Crimes463(SC), MANU/SC/0896/2020

Case note: Criminal - Transfer of Trial - Section 406 of the Code of Criminal Procedure, 1973 (CrPC) read with Order XXXIX of the Supreme Court Rules - Accused alleged sacrilege of the holy book - Bias and prejudice apprehended - Accused contended unlikely of getting fair trial in the face of strong presumption of culpability - Whether fair trial an impossibility, before the Courts in Punjab or the present is a case of mere apprehension by the Accused?

Facts: The instant matter related to alleged sacrilege of the holy book, Shri Guru Granth Sahibji in the year 2015 different places in Punjab that caused deep anguish and bitterness amongst a particular religious group forming majority of the population in the State of Punjab. Accused members of the Dera Sacha Sauda sect contended to have been facing bias and prejudice and thus unlikely to get a fair trial in the face of strong presumption of culpability. Petitioners sought transfer of trials in various cases for adjudication. Accused person also cited threat implication.

Hon'ble Apex Court held, while dismissing the petition:

Here the projection of surcharged atmosphere is not borne out by the corresponding reaction of the Petitioners, who are out on bail. Being residents of Punjab, they continue to reside at their usual place and are going about their routine affairs. If their threat perceptions were genuine, they could not have gone about their normal ways. For this reason, the Court is inclined to believe that the atmosphere in the State does not justify shifting of the trial venue to another State.

For transfer of trial from one Court to another, the Court must be fully satisfied about existence of such factors which would make it impossible to conduct a fair trial. General allegation of surcharged atmosphere is not however sufficient. The apprehension of not getting a fair and impartial trial cannot be founded on certain grievances or convenience of the Accused but the reasons have to be more compelling than that. One must also be mindful of the fact that when trial is shifted out from one State to another, it would tantamount to Â casting aspersions on the Court, having lawful jurisdiction to try Â the case. Hence powers under Section 406 Â Code of Criminal Procedure must be exercised sparingly and only in deserving cases when fair and impartial trial uninfluenced by external factors, is not at all possible.[11]

Petitioners, who are out on bail, being residents of Punjab, continue to reside at their usual place and are going about their routine affairs. If their 24-06-2021 threat perceptions were genuine, they could not have gone about their normal ways. For this reason, the Court is inclined to believe that the atmosphere in the State does not justify shifting of the trial venue to another State.[13]

The sacrilege Â incidents occurred in 2015 and it has been more than 2 years since the Petitioners were arrayed as Accused in the cases. During this long period, no complaint was made by the Petitioners of any threat to their security or to their associates. Barring one issue, none of the Petitioners raised any grievances before the court or before the police and Â inference Â must accordingly will have to be drawn against their transfer plea.[15]

From the available material, this Court cannot reasonably conclude that the situation in Punjab is not conducive for a fair trial for the Petitioners. [18]

Moreover, it cannot just be the convenience of the Petitioner but also of the Complainant, the Witnesses, the prosecution. The larger issue of trial normally being conducted by the jurisdictional Court must also weigh on the issue. When relative convenience and difficulties of all the parties involved in the process are taken into account, no credible case for transfer of trial to alternative venues outside the State of Punjab made out.[19]

The transfer of trial from one state to another would inevitably reflect on the credibility of the State's judiciary. Except for compelling factors and Â clear situation of deprivation of fair justice, the transfer power should not be invoked. [21]

Present cases found devoid of merit. [22]

• • •

CHAPTER V

National Alliance for People's Movements and Ors. Vs. The State of Maharashtra and Ors., 2020

Relevant Sections:

- The Constitution of India- article 14

Hon'ble judges:S.A. Bobde, C.J.I., A.S. Bopanna and V. Ramasubramanian, JJ.

No. of pdf pages in Original Judgment: 7

Equivalent Citations:2020(216)AIC5, AIR2020SC4448, 2020ALLMR(Cri)3723, 2020(6)BLJ316, 2020(4)Crimes72(SC), MANU/SC/0702/2020, (2020)9SCC698, 2020 (7-8) SCJ 571

Case note: Criminal - Release of prisoners - Unprecedented Circumstances due to Pandemic - High Powered Committee formed at state level to categorise temporary release - Petitioners sought clarifications and requested forexclusion of certain categories in the form of clarification - High Court videimpugned findings refused to interfere with the orders of High PoweredCommittee.

Facts: The Petitioners moved before High Court claiming to be in Public Interest seeking that the decision of the High Powered Committee ('HPC') dated 25.03.2020 to the extent of relevant clauses of HPC meeting dated 11.05.2020 excluding certain categories of offences as provided in relevant paragraphs for the purpose of grant of interim bail and corrigendum dated 18.05.2020 of the Minutes of the Meeting of HPC dated 11.05.2020 to the extent of clarification that the class and/or category of offences determined for temporary release be not read as a direction made by it for mandatory release of prisoners falling in that category or class and a further clarification that the case of every prisoner be considered on case to case basis for deciding the temporary release of such prisoners. The Petitioners also sought for a direction to the Respondents to release the prisoners convicted for life imprisonment without insisting that they were released in the past at least twice, either on furlough or parole. The High Court declined to interfere with decision of the HPC and hence the present petition.

Hon'ble Apex Court held, while dismissing the appeals:

The entire right to claim such interim bail has arisen in the unprecedented circumstance of the pandemic and the consideration for interim bail is not in the nature of a statutory right for bail based on other legal consideration but is more in the nature of human right to safeguard the health. The provision for bail as otherwise provided in law in any case would be considered by the competent courts if such right for bail is made out before the competent court irrespective of the pandemic or not. The present option provided is only as a solution to help decongestion and to avoid the spread of virus.

The very purpose of directing each of the States/Union Territories to constitute a High-Powered Committee is that the HPC taking note of the subsisting position in such State will take a decision in the matter as the HPC will have the wherewithal to secure all details and take a decision. If the said aspect is kept in view, it is noticed that by the guideline dated 25.03.2020 the Committee in question has categorised the undertrials/convicted persons by the nature of the crime and the length of the punishment which will take care of the severity in the process of consideration. In that regard, insofar as the undertrial/convicted persons charged under the common law, namely, the Indian Penal Code; they are classified into two categories i.e. category-(i) as punishment below 7 years and category-(ii) as punishment above 7 years so that the consideration could be in that manner. The Committee has thought it fit to separately classify the undertrials/convicted persons who are charged under the Special Enactments irrespective of the duration of imprisonment notwithstanding the fact that the punishment imposed could be less than 7 years. In that regard, what has weighed with the HPC is that such enactments provide for additional restrictions on grant of bail in addition to those under the Code of Criminal Procedure. The said categorisation cannot be considered as unreasonable since at the first instance, based on the categorisation made a consideration is required by the Court for grant of interim bail if such undertrial/convicted person is seeking bail purely on taking benefit of the notification issued pursuant to such decision taken by the HPC. The exclusion made has a reasonable basis and cannot be termed arbitrary.

Having stated so it is necessary to indicate that the cause for grievance may arise for an individual undertrial/convicted prisoner only if such person has been discriminated as against the prisoner in the same category for which the benefit has been provided by the categorisation made by the

The Single Judge dismissed the application for anticipatory bail by holding that the alleged irregularities committed by the Appellant makes out a prima facie case for refusing pre-arrest bail to the Appellant.

Hon'ble Apex Court held, while dismissing the appeal:(i) In terms of Section 4 of the PMLA, the offence of money-laundering was punishable with rigorous imprisonment for a term not less than three years extending to seven years and with fine. The Second Schedule to the Code of Criminal Procedure relates to classification of offences against other laws and in terms of the Second Schedule of the Code, an offence which is punishable with imprisonment for three years and upward but not more than seven years is a cognizable and non-bailable offence. Thus, Section 4 of the Act read with the Second Schedule of the Code makes it clear that the offences under the PMLA are cognizable offences. Section 420 of Indian Penal Code, Section 8 of the Prevention of Corruption Act was then found a mention in Part A of the Schedule. Section 420 Indian Penal Code, Section 8 of the Prevention of Corruption Act is punishable for a term extending to seven years. Thus, the essential requirement of Section 45 of PMLA Accused of an offence punishable for a term of imprisonment of more than three years under Part A of the Schedule was satisfied making the offence under PMLA. There was no merit in the contention of the Appellant that very registration of the FIR against the Appellant under PMLA was not maintainable.

(ii) As rightly submitted by Respondent that if the Accused were to be confronted with the materials which were collected by the prosecution/ Enforcement Directorate with huge efforts, it would lead to devastating consequences and would defeat the very purpose of the investigation into crimes, in particular, white collar offences. If the contention of the Appellant was to be accepted, the investigating agency would have to question each and every Accused such materials collected during investigation and in this process, the investigating agency would be exposing the evidence collected by them with huge efforts using their men and resources and this would give a chance to the Accused to tamper with the evidence and to destroy the money trail apart from paving the way for the Accused to influence the witnesses. If the contention of the Appellant was to be accepted that the Accused would have to be questioned with the materials and the investigating agency has to satisfy the court that the Accused was evasive during interrogation, the court would have to undertake a mini trial of scrutinizing the matter at intermediary stages of investigation like interrogation of the Accused and the answers elicited from the Accused and to find out whether the answers given by the Accused are evasive or whether they were satisfactory or not. This could have never been the intention of the legislature either under PMLA or any other statute.

(iii) Grant of anticipatory bail at the stage of investigation may frustrate the investigating agency in interrogating the Accused and in collecting the useful information and also the materials which might have been concealed. Success in such interrogation would elude if the Accused knows that he is protected by the order of the court. Grant of anticipatory bail, particularly in economic offences would definitely hamper the effective investigation. Having regard to the materials said to have been collected by the Respondent-Enforcement Directorate and considering the stage of the investigation, this court was of the view that it was not a fit case to grant anticipatory bail.

(iv) In a case of money-laundering where it involves many stages of placement, layering i.e. funds moved to other institutions to conceal origin and interrogation i.e. funds used to acquire various assets, it requires systematic and analysed investigation which would be of great advantage. As held in case of Anil Sharma, success in such interrogation would elude if the Accused knows that he is protected by a pre-arrest bail order. Section 438 Code of Criminal Procedure is to be invoked only in exceptional cases where the case alleged is frivolous or groundless. In the case in hand, there were allegations of laundering the proceeds of the crime. The Enforcement Directorate claims to have certain specific inputs from various sources, including overseas banks. Letter rogatory was also said to have been issued and some response have been received by the department. Having regard to the nature of allegations and the stage of the investigation, the investigating agency had to be given sufficient freedom in the process of investigation. Though this court did not endorse the approach of the Single Judge in extracting the note produced by the Enforcement Directorate, there was no ground warranting interference with the impugned order. Considering the facts and circumstances of the case, grant of anticipatory bail to the Appellant would hamper the investigation and this was not a fit case for exercise of discretion to grant anticipatory bail to the Appellant.

Ratio Decidendi: Grant of anticipatory bail, particularly in economic offences would definitely hamper the effective investigation.

● ● ●

CHAPTER VII

Prathvi Raj Chauhan Vs. Union of India (UOI) and Ors. 2020

Relevant Sections: Scheduled Castes And The Scheduled Tribes (Prevention Of Atrocities) Act, 1989 - Section 18; Scheduled Castes And The Scheduled Tribes (Prevention Of Atrocities) Act, 1989 - Section 18A; Code of Criminal Procedure, 1973 (CrPC) - Section 438

Hon'ble judges: Arun Mishra, Vineet Saran and S. Ravindra Bhat, JJ.

No. of pdf pages in Original Judgment: 24

Equivalent Citations: 2020(213)AIC80, AIR2020SC1036, 2020 (113) ACC 307, 2021 1 AWC795SC, 2020(3)ALD17, 2020 (1) ALD(Crl.) 693 (SC), 2020(4)CTC906, 129(2020)CLT801, 2020(2)JLJ384, 2020 (2) KHC 423, 2020(1)KLJ718, 2020(1)KLT810, 2020(1)MLJ(Crl)378 , MANU/SC/0157/2020, 2020(I)OLR419, (2020)4SCC727, 2020 (6) SCJ 449, (2020)1WBLR(SC)649

Case note: Criminal - Anticipatory bail - Validity of provision - Sections 18A and 18A(i) of Scheduled Castes and Scheduled Tribes Act, 1989 and Sections 438 and 482 of Code of Criminal Procedure, 1973 - Petitioners had questioned provisions inserted by way of carving out Section 18A of Act, 1989 dealing with applicability of Section 438 of Code, preliminary inquiry and approval of arrest in relation with persons committing offence under 1989 Act - It had been submitted that this Court had noted in Dr. Subhash Kashinath that provisions of Act of 1989 are being misused as such amendment was arbitrary, unjust, irrational and violative of Article 21 of Constitution of India - Hence, present petition - Whether Section 18A of Act was arbitrary, unjust, irrational and of Article 21 of Constitution of India.

Facts: The Petitioners had questioned the provisions inserted by way of carving out Section 18A of the Scheduled Castes and Scheduled Tribes Act, 1989 (Act of 1989) dealing with applicability of Section 438 of Code, preliminary inquiry and approval of arrest in relation with persons committing offence under 1989 Act. It was submitted that Section 18A had been enacted to nullify the judgment of this Court in Dr. Subhash Kashinath Mahajan v. The State of Maharashtra and Anr. It had been submitted that there could not have been any curtailment of the right to obtain anticipatory bail under Section 438 Code of Criminal Procedure Prior scrutiny and proper investigation are necessary. Most of the safeguards had been provided under the Act of 1989 to prevent undue harassment.

Hon'ble Apex Court held, while disposing off the appeal:

Arun Mishra, J.

(i) Concerning the provisions contained in Section 18A, suffice it to observe that with respect to preliminary inquiry for registration of FIR, we have already recalled the general directions issued in Dr. Subhash Kashinath's case. A preliminary inquiry is permissible only in the circumstances as per the law laid down by a Constitution Bench of this Court in Lalita Kumari v. Government of U.P., shall hold good as explained in the order passed by this Court in the review petitions and the amended provisions of Section 18A have to be interpreted accordingly.

(ii) The Section 18A(i) was inserted owing to the decision of this Court in Dr. Subhash Kashinath, which made it necessary to obtain the approval of the appointing authority concerning a public servant and the SSP in the case of arrest of Accused persons. This Court has also recalled that direction on Review Petition. Thus, the provisions which had been made in Section 18A were rendered of academic use as they were enacted to take care of mandate issued in Dr. Subhash Kashinath which no more prevails. The provisions were already in Section 18 of the Act with respect to anticipatory bail.

(iii) Concerning the applicability of provisions of Section 438 Code of Criminal Procedure, it shall not apply to the cases under Act of 1989. However, if the complaint did not make out a prima facie case for applicability of the provisions of the Act of 1989, the bar created by Section 18 and 18A(i) shall not apply.

(iv) The court could, in exceptional cases, exercise power under Section 482 Code of Criminal Procedure for quashing the cases to prevent misuse of provisions on settled parameters, as already observed while deciding the review petitions. The legal position was clear, and no argument to the contrary had been raised.

S. Ravindra Bhat, J.

(i) It was important to keep oneself reminded that while sometimes (perhaps mostly in urban areas) false accusations were made, those were not necessarily reflective of the prevailing and wide spread social prejudices against members of these oppressed classes. Significantly, the amendment of 2016, in the expanded definition of atrocity, also lists pernicious practices including forcing the eating of inedible matter, dumping of excreta near the homes or in the neighbourhood of members of such communities and several other forms of humiliation, which members of such scheduled caste communities are subjected to. All these considerations far outweigh the Petitioners' concern that innocent individuals would be subjected to what are described as arbitrary processes of investigation and legal proceedings, without adequate safeguards. The right to a trial with all attendant safeguards are available to those Accused of committing offences under the Act, they remain unchanged by the enactment of the amendment.

(ii) While considering any application seeking pre-arrest bail, the High Court had to balance the two interests: i.e. that the power was not so used as to convert the jurisdiction into that under Section 438 of the Code of Criminal Procedure, but that it was used sparingly and such orders made in very exceptional cases where no prima facie offence was made out as shown in the FIR, and further also that if such orders were not made in those classes of cases, the result would inevitably be a miscarriage of justice or abuse of process of law.

• • •

CHAPTER VIII

Saravanan Vs. State represented by the Inspector of Police, 2020

Relevant Sections:

- Code of Criminal Procedure, 1973 (CrPC) - Section 437, Section 167(2)

Hon'ble judges: Ashok Bhushan, R. Subhash Reddy and M.R. Shah, JJ.

No. of pdf pages in Original Judgment: 6

Equivalent Citations: 2020(216)AIC1, AIR2020SC5010, 2021 (114) ACC 256, 2021 (1) ALT (Crl.) 34 (A.P.), 2021 (1) ALD(Crl.) 560 (SC), 2020(6)BLJ516, 2020(4)Crimes117(SC), 131(2021)CLT201, 2020(5)JKJ264[SC], 2020(4)MLJ(Crl)413, MANU/SC/0764/2020, 2020(II)OLR1005, 2020(4)RLW3091(SC), (2020)9SCC101

Case note: Criminal - Release on Default/ Statutory Bail - Section 167(2) of the Code of Criminal Procedure, 1973 (CrPC) - No charge sheet filed within stipulated time period - Previous bail applications under Section 437 CrPC were denied - Statutory bail claimed denied due to non-compliance of condition of deposit made in regular bail application - Whether while releasing the Accused on default bail/statutory bail under Section 167(2), any condition of deposit of amount as imposed by the High Court, could have been imposed?

Facts: The present appeal is against the order granting release on default or statutory bail. The Appellant was arrested and remanded to the judicial custody for the offences punishable under Section 420 of the IPC. Appellant was granted bail based on assurance to repay the amount due as per affidavit filed by wife of the Appellant. Appellant as per the order was directed to repay one portion now and balance by date stipulated therein. This order was challenged by Appellant before the High Court. The High Court dismissed the said application with liberty to the Appellant to approach the Magistrate Court for any modification and observed that if any modification is required, the same may be considered by the Magistrate. Appellant thereafter filed an application before the learned Sessions Court claiming default bail/statutory bail under Section 167(2), Code of Criminal Procedure on the ground that prosecution failed to complete the investigation as per law. Sessions Court dismissed the application on the ground of Appellant's failure in complying with the previous conditional bail order. In appeal, the High Court, by the impugned judgment accepted the same, however, considering the earlier undertaking given by Appellant's wife imposed the condition on Appellant to make a deposit of sum mentioned therein. Hence, the present appeals.

Hon'ble Apex Court held, while allowing the appeal: High Court committed a grave error in imposing condition that the Appellant shall deposit a sum of Rs. 8,00,000/- while releasing the Appellant on default bail/statutory bail. It appears that the High Court has imposed such a condition taking into consideration the fact that earlier at the time of hearing of the regular bail application, before the learned Magistrate, the wife of the Appellant filed an affidavit agreeing to deposit Rs. 7,00,000/-. However, where the investigation is not completed within 60 days or 90 days, as the case may be, and no chargesheet is filed by 60th or 90th day, Accused gets an "indefeasible right" to default bail, and the Accused becomes entitled to default bail once the Accused applies for default bail and furnish bail. Therefore, the only requirement for getting the default bail/statutory bail Under Section 167(2), Code of Criminal Procedure is that the Accused is in jail for more than 60 or 90 days, as the case may be, and within 60 or 90 days, as the case may be, the investigation is not completed and no chargesheet is filed by 60th or 90th day and the Accused applies for default bail and is prepared to furnish bail. No other condition of deposit of the alleged amount involved can be imposed. Imposing such condition while releasing the Accused on default bail/statutory bail would frustrate the very object and purpose of default bail Under Section 167(2), Code of Criminal Procedure.

The circumstances while considering the regular bail application under Section 437 Code of Criminal Procedure are different, while considering the application for default bail/statutory bail.

The present appeals succeed. Condition directing the Appellant to deposit quashed and set aside. Condition directing the Appellant to report before the concerned police station at 10:00 a.m. daily, until further orders for interrogation is hereby modified to the extent and it is directed that the Appellant shall co-operate with the investigating agency and shall report the concerned police station as and when called for investigation/interrogation and on non-cooperation, the consequences including cancellation of the bail shall follow.

The appeals are allowed accordingly.

Ratio Decidendi- Circumstances while considering regular bail application under Section 437 Code of Criminal Procedure, 1973 (Code) are different than one while considering application for default bail/statutory bail under Section 167(2) of the Code.

∴

CHAPTER IX

SumetiVij Vs. Paramount Tech Fab Industries, 2021

Relevant Sections:

- Negotiable Instruments Act, 1881 - Section 138, 139

Hon'ble judges: Indu Malhotra and Ajay Rastogi, JJ.
No. of pdf pages in Original Judgment: 9
Equivalent Citations: AIR2021SC1281, 2021CriLJ1587, 2021(2)CTC579, MANU/SC/0167/2021, 2021(1)RLW690(SC), 2021(2)RCR(Criminal)331

Case note: Criminal - Cheque dishonour - Section 138 of the Negotiable Instruments Act, 1881 (Act) - Findings of acquittal reversed by Impugned Judgment - Trial Court held that complainant failed to prove the case - High Court however held otherwise and set aside the order of acquittal - Hence, the present appeal -Whether in the absence of the prima-facie burden being discharged by complainant, mere issuance of the cheques sufficient to justify that cheques were issued in discharge of any debt or other liability?

Facts: Cheque issued in a sale transaction by Appellant dishonoured due to insufficient funds. Two legal notices were sent by the complainant to the Appellant, however were neither responded nor any payment was made. Two separate complaints were filed against the Appellant-Accused. Trial Judge returned a finding that the complainant failed to establish that the material/goods were delivered to the Appellant in lieu of which, the cheques were issued, and in the absence of burden being discharged by the complainant, the onus to disprove or rebut the presumption could not be shifted to the Appellant as referred under Section 139 of the Act. High Court on reappraisal of the evidence on record affirmed that the primary burden was discharged by the complainant and set aside the finding of acquittal recorded by trial Judge. Hence, the present appeal.

Hon'ble Apex Court held, while dismissing the appeal: In the instant case, the Appellant has only recorded her statement Under Section 313 of the Code, and has not adduced any evidence to rebut the presumption that the cheques were issued for consideration. Once the facts came on record remained unrebutted and supported with the evidence on record with no substantive evidence of defence of the Appellant to explain the incriminating circumstances appearing in the complaint against her, no error committed by the High Court in the impugned judgment, and the Appellant rightly convicted for the offence punishable under Section 138 of the Act and needs no interference of this Court.

That apart, when the complainant exhibited all these documents in support of his complaints and recorded the statement of three witnesses in support thereof, the Appellant has recorded her statement under Section 313 of the Code, but failed to record evidence to disprove or rebut the presumption in support of her defence available Under Section 139 of the Act. The statement of the Accused recorded Under Section 313 of the Code is not a substantive evidence of defence, but only an opportunity to the Accused to explain the incriminating circumstances appearing in the prosecution case of the Accused. Therefore, there is no evidence to rebut the presumption that the cheques were issued for consideration.

In the given circumstances, the High Courthas not committed any error in recording the finding of guilt of the Appellant and convicting her for an offence being committed under Section 138 of the Act under its impugned judgment, which needs no further interference. Consequently, the appeals dismissed.

• • •

CHAPTER X

The State of Kerala Vs. Mahesh, 2021

Relevant Sections:

- CRPC-s. 438,439
- IPC-302,307,324,341

Hon'ble judges: Indira Banerjee and Krishna Murari, JJ.
No. of pdf pages in Original Judgment: 13
Equivalent Citations: 2021(2)MLJ(Crl)205, MANU/SC/0232/2021

Case note: Criminal - Bail - Cancelation of - Sections 302, 307, 324 and 341 of Indian Penal Code, 1860 - Respondent Accused stabbed victim, with knife, inside multispeciality dental clinic, run by victim - FIR was lodged under Sections 341, 324 and 307 of Code - However, after death of the victim, Section 302 was added - Bail application filed by Respondent Accused in Sessions Court was dismissed - Respondent Accused filed bail application in High Court - High Court had granted bail to Respondent Accused - Hence, present appeal - Whether High Court erred in granting bail to Respondent accused.

Facts: The Respondent Accused stabbed the victim, with a knife, inside a multi-speciality dental clinic, run by the victim. An FIR was lodged under Sections 341, 324 and 307 of the Indian Penal code (IPC). However, after the death of the victim, Section 302 was added and an Inclusion Report to that effect was filed in the Jurisdictional Court. The crime had been registered under Sections 341, 324, 201, 212, 307 and 302 of the Indian Penal Code. A Bail application filed by the Respondent Accused in the Sessions Court was dismissed. The Respondent Accused filed the bail application in the High Court. The prayer for bail was strongly opposed by the Public Prosecutor who argued that, if released, the Respondent Accused would influence witnesses many of whom were his close relatives, friends and acquaintances. The High Court has however, granted bail to the Respondent Accused, by the order impugned in this appeal, notwithstanding the opposition of the Public Prosecutor, overlooking the materials on record, which prima facie indicate that the Respondent had committed cold blooded murder of a young lady doctor, as a fall out of a soured relationship.

Hon'ble Apex court held, while allowing the appeal: (i) The impugned order of the High Court was flawed, in that the High Court noted the seriousness of the offence alleged, observed that the incident was heinous, but proceeded to grant bail to the Respondent Accused on the purported ground that he had been in custody without even considering the materials on record which prima facie made out reasonable grounds to believe that the Respondent Accused had committed the heinous offence. At that stage, even the chargesheet had not been filed. The High Court did not apply its mind to the severity of the punishment in the event of conviction, or the fact that the Accused had been absconding after the incident.

(ii) As argued on behalf of the Appellant, supported by the applicant for intervention, being the hapless parent of the victim, the High Court had neither considered nor discussed the elaborate reasons given by the Sessions Court in its order rejecting the prayer of the Respondent Accused for bail. The impugned order of the High Court did not advert to any error in the reasoning of the Sessions Court. Nor was there any discussion of the reason why the High Court took a view different from that taken by the Sessions Court-whether there were any supervening circumstances within ten or twelve days of the order of the Sessions Court, which necessitated a different view.

(iii) The High Court, clearly erred in not appreciating that the apprehension of the Prosecution that the Respondent Accused would influence witnesses, could not be put to rest, by directing the Respondent Accused not to enter the jurisdiction of Police Station. The High Court completely ignored the fact that the deceased victim used to reside at Ernakulam. Her parents and her five years old daughter reside at Ernakulam. In other words, the only eye witness was a resident of Ernakulam. Most of the Prosecution witnesses were from Thrissur. There was no reason to suppose that the witnesses would restrict their movements to the limits of the jurisdiction of Police Station.

(iv) The impugned order of the High Court was set aside.

• • •

CHAPTER XI

Aparna Bhat and Ors Vs State of Madhya Pradesh, 2021

Relevant Sections:
CRPC-S.438
IPC-S.452,354A,323,506
Hon'ble judges: A.M. Khanwilkar and S. Ravindra Bhat, JJ.
No. of pdf pages in Original Judgment: 18
Equivalent Citations: AIR2021SC1492, MANU/SC/0193/2021

Case note: Criminal - Bail conditions - Validity of - Accused-applicant, neighbour of complainant, entered her house and caught hold of complainant's hand, and allegedly attempted to harass her sexually - Crime was registered for offences punishable under Sections 452, 354A, 323 and 506 of Code - Case was investigated and charge sheet was filed - Accused filed application under Section 438 of Code seeking pre-arrest bail - High Court while granting bail to applicant imposed condition that applicant along with his wife shall visit house of complainant with Rakhi thread/band with box of sweets and request complainant to tie Rakhi band to him with promise to protect her - Hence, present appeal - Whether bail conditions imposed by High Court liable to set aside.

Facts: The Accused-applicant, neighbour of the complainant, entered her house and caught hold of the complainant's hand, and allegedly attempted to harass her sexually. Accordingly, Crime was registered for the offences punishable under Sections 452, 354A, 323 and 506 of the Indian Penal Code (IPC). The case was investigated and a charge sheet was filed. The Accused filed an application under Section 438 of Code of Criminal Procedure, 1973 seeking pre-arrest bail. The High Court, by the impugned order, even while granting bail to the applicant imposed the condition that the applicant along with his wife shall visit the house of the complainant with Rakhi thread/band with a box of sweets and request the complainant to tie the Rakhi band to him with the promise to protect her to the best of his ability.

Hon'ble Apex court held, while allowing the appeal: (i) The use of reasoning/language which diminishes the offence and tends to trivialize the survivor, was especially to be avoided under all circumstances. Thus, the following conduct, actions or situations were hereby deemed irrelevant, e.g. - to say that the survivor had in the past consented to such or similar acts or that she behaved promiscuously, or by her acts or clothing, provoked the alleged action of the Accused, that she behaved in a manner unbecoming of chaste or Indian women, or that she had called upon the situation by her behaviour, etc. These instances were only illustrations of an attitude which should never enter judicial verdicts or orders or be considered relevant while making a judicial decision; they could not be reasons for granting bail or other such relief. Similarly, imposing conditions that implicitly tend to condone or diminish the harm caused by the Accused and have the effect of potentially exposing the survivor to secondary trauma, such as mandating mediation processes in non-compoundable offences, mandating as part of bail conditions, community service (in a manner of speaking with the so-called reformative approach towards the perpetrator of sexual offence) or requiring tendering of apology once or repeatedly, or in any manner getting or being in touch with the survivor, was especially forbidden. The law did not permit or countenance such conduct, where the survivor could potentially be traumatized many times over or be led into some kind of non-voluntary acceptance, or be compelled by the circumstances to accept and condone behavior what was a serious offence.

(ii) The courts should desist from expressing any stereotype opinion, in words spoken during proceedings, or in the course of a judicial order, to the effect that (i) women are physically weak and need protection (ii) women are incapable of or cannot take decisions on their own, (iii) men are the head of the household and should take all the decisions relating to family (iv) women should be submissive and obedient according to our culture; (v) good women are sexually chaste (vi) motherhood is the duty and role of every woman, and assumptions to the effect that she wants to be a mother (vii) women should be the ones in charge of their children, their upbringing and care (viii) being alone at night or wearing certain clothes make women responsible for being attacked (ix) a woman consuming alcohol, smoking, etc. may justify unwelcome advances by men or has asked for it (x) women are emotional and often overreact or dramatize events, hence it is necessary to corroborate their testimony (xi) testimonial evidence provided by women who are sexually active may be suspected when assessing consent in sexual offence cases; and (xii) lack of evidence of physical harm in sexual offence case leads to an inference of consent by the woman.

(iii) Therefore, the bail conditions in the impugned judgment, were set aside, and expunged from the record.

∙ ∙ ∙

CHAPTER XII

Girraj vs Kiranpal and Ors,2021

Relevant Sections:

- IPC- sections 147,148,149,302,307,323,342 and 502
- ARMS ACT- s.27, 30

Hon'ble judges: Dr. D.Y. Chandrachud and M.R. Shah, JJ.
No. of pdf pages in Original Judgment: 7
EquivalentCitations:
AIR2021SC1484, MANU/SC/0178/2021, 2021(2)RCR(Criminal)317

Case note: Criminal - Cancellation of bail - Sections 147, 148, 149, 302, 307, 323, 342 and 508 of Indian Penal Code, 1860 - First information report registered against the Accused under Sections 147, 148, 149, 302, 307, 323, 342 and 508 of Code - Pursuant to registration of FIR, investigation by police was completed and charge sheet was filed against all Accused - High Court granted bail to Respondent-Accused - Hence, present appeal - Whether bail granted to Respondent-accused liable to cancelled.

Facts: An First information report registered against the Accused under Sections 147, 148, 149, 302, 307, 323, 342 and 508 of the Indian Penal Code 1860. Pursuant to the registration of the FIR, the investigation by the police was completed and a charge sheet was filed under Sections 147, 148, 149, 307, 323, 326, 341 and 506 of the Indian Penal Code 1860 against all the Accused and under Section 27 and 30 of the Arms Act. The first order granting bail was in the case of co-Accused. All the other Accused while claiming the grant of bail had specifically relied upon the order passed in the case of said co accused and sought bail on the basis of parity. Following the principle of parity, the High Court enlarged them on bail.

Hon'ble Apex court held, while allowing the appeal: (i) Ex facie, the orders of the High Court would indicate that the only basis for claiming bail in the present batch of cases was by placing reliance on the order granting bail to the co-Accused. The bail which had been granted to said co accused had been cancelled by the order of this Court. Nonetheless, in order to ensure fairness to the co-Accused, who are the Respondents in these proceedings, it would be appropriate to furnish them an opportunity to apply for bail before the High Court, conditional on their surrendering in pursuance of the order which we propose to pass cancelling their bail.

• • •

CHAPTER XIII

Kanakarajan vs State of Kerala, 2017

Relevant Sections:

- IPC-Sections 143, 148, 302 and 342
- CRPC- Section 313

Hon'ble judges: *N.V. Ramana and Prafulla C. Pant, JJ.*
No. of pdf pages in Original Judgment: 7

Equivalent Citations: AIR2017SC2779, 2017 (100) ACC 285, 2017(2)ACR1297, 2017 (2) ALD(Crl.) 297 (SC), 2017(3)BomCR(Cri)73, 2017(2)Crimes362(SC), III(2017)CCR20(SC), 124(2017)CLT417, 2017(3)J.L.J.R.26, 2017(2)JCC1458, MANU/SC/0472/2017, 2017(3)N.C.C.352, 2017(II)OLR299, 2017(3)PLJR154, 2017(4)RLW2770(SC), 2017(3)RCR(Criminal)417, 2017(5)SCALE158, (2017)13SCC597, 2017 (5) SCJ 564, 2017(2)UC1149

Case note: Criminal - Conviction - Appreciation of evidence - Sections 143, 148, 302 and 342 of Indian Penal Code, 1860 - Nine Accused against whom FIR was registered for causing death of deceased and injuring cousin of deceased - Since A2 was found dead, charges were framed only against remaining Accused - Trial Court acquitted A3, A4, A6, A7, A8 and A9 of charges - Convicted Appellant/A1 and A5 for offences punishable under Sections 143, 148, 342 and 302 of Code - High Court acquitted A5 of all charges but upheld order of conviction as against Appellant - Hence, present appeal - Whether impugned order was sustainable

Facts: The Accused persons attacked the deceased, with deadly weapons such as swords and sticks, as a result of which he sustained grievous injuries. When the complainant/PW2 tried to intervene and stop the Accused, he too was beaten up by the Accused. The Trial Court came to the conclusion that the prosecution could not prove the guilt of Accused A3, A4, A6, A7, A8 and A9 beyond reasonable doubt and acquitted them by extending the benefit of doubt. However, the Trial Court found A1 and A5 guilty of the offences Under Sections 143, 148, 302 and 342 of Indian Penal Code, 1860. The High Court gave benefit of doubt to A5 and allowed his appeal by acquitting him of the offences charged. The appeal of Appellant/A1 was however dismissed by the High Court as being devoid of any merit, thereby confirming the order of conviction and sentence passed by the Trial Court. Hence, the present appeal.

Hon'ble Apex court held, while allowing the appeal: (i) There were certain pivotal issues where the prosecution failed to provide a satisfactory explanation. There was no investigation or explanation put forth by the prosecution for the injuries. The witnesses were not cogent and trustworthy to form basis to convict the Appellant. Admittedly the incident had taken place in the midst of several hundred people and the prosecution witnesses in equivocal terms stated that the police personnel were present. The prosecution had not taken minimum care to examine the independent witnesses in support of their case and particularly when it was nobody's case that independent witnesses were not available.

(ii) The High Court, while convicting the Appellant, should have been more cautious while weighing the evidence of the prosecution witnesses. Non-explanation of the serious injuries on the body of the Accused A2 by the prosecution was fatal. The High Court while convicting the Accused overlooked settled principles of criminal law and in a mechanical way based its conclusion on the premise that the injuries were not sustained in the process of the same incident. There was non-conduction of the test identification parade. The impugned judgement was set aside.

• • •

CHAPTER XIV

Naveen Singh Vs The State of Uttar Pradesh, 2021

Relevant Sections:

- IPC- Section 120-B,420,467,468,471

Hon'ble judges: *Dr. D.Y. Chandrachud and M.R. Shah, JJ.*
No. of pdf pages in Original Judgment: 9

Equivalent Citations: AIR2017SC2779, 2017 (100) ACC 285, 2017(2)ACR1297, 2017 (2) ALD(Crl.) 297 (SC), 2017(3)BomCR(Cri)73, 2017(2)Crimes362(SC), III(2017)CCR20(SC), 124(2017)CLT417, 2017(3)J.L.J.R.26, 2017(2)JCC1458, MANU/SC/0472/2017, 2017(3)N.C.C.352, 2017(II)OLR299, 2017(3)PLJR154, 2017(4)RLW2770(SC), 2017(3)RCR(Criminal)417, 2017(5)SCALE158, (2017)13SCC597, 2017 (5) SCJ 564, 2017(2)UC1149

Case note: Criminal - Bail - Cancellation of - Sections 120-B, 420, 467, 468 and 471 of Indian Penal Code, 1860 - Record Keeper of Civil Court on order of District Judge had lodged FIR against Respondent No. 2 for offences under Sections 420, 467, 468, 471, 120-B of Code for committing forgery in Court record - Respondent No. 2 filed application for regular bail before Sessions Court - Additional Sessions Judge dismissed said bail application observing that allegations against Accused were very serious of forging court's records and that Accused was beneficiary of said forgery and therefore this was not fit case to release him on bail - Thereafter Respondent No. 2-Accused approached High Court - High Court had released Respondent No. 2-Accused on bail - Hence, present appeal - Whether impugned order passed by High Court releasing Respondent No. 2-Accused on bail was sustainable.

Facts: A writ petition was filed by the Appellant before the High Court for issuance of writ of mandamus to take action on the complaint made by him against Respondent No. 2 for committing forgery in Court record. Additional Sessions Judge sent his comments/enquiry report indicating that the judicial record pertaining to Sessions Trial under Sections 307, 504 and 506 Indian Penal Code was tampered with. The High Court directed District and Sessions Judge to take notice of the record and ensure that the needful was done. Thereafter on the order of the District and Sessions Judge, the Record keeper had lodged the said FIR against Respondent No. 2 for the offences. The Record Keeper of the Civil Court on the order of the District Judge had lodged an FIR against Respondent No. 2 for the offences under Sections 420, 467, 468, 471, 120-B Indian Penal Code. Respondent No. 2-Accused filed an application for regular bail before the Sessions Court. The Additional Sessions Judge dismissed the said bail application observing that the allegations against the Accused are very serious of forging the court's records and that the Accused was the beneficiary of the said forgery and therefore this was not a fit case to release him on bail. That thereafter Respondent No. 2-Accused approached the High Court. The High Court had released Respondent No. 2-Accused on bail.

Hon'ble Apex court held, while allowing the appeal: (i) It appears that High Court has not adverted itself to the seriousness of the case and the offences alleged against Respondent No. 2-Accused and the gravity of the matter. From the impugned order, it appears that the High Court has released Respondent No. 2-Accused on bail in a routine and casual manner and without adverting to the seriousness of the offence and the gravity of the matter relating to forgery and/or manipulating the court order. From the impugned judgment and order passed by the High Court, it appears that High Court had only observed that since the innocence and complicity of the Accused could be decided only after taking evidence with regard thereto, without commenting anything on merit as to the complicity, involvement and severeness of the offences, the case being triable by the Magistrate and the charge sheet having been filed and the Accused was languishing in jail, was entitled to be released on bail. However, the High Court had not at all considered that the Accused is charged for the offences under Sections 420, 467, 468, 471, 120-B Indian Penal Code and the maximum punishment for offence under Section 467 Indian Penal Code is ten years and fine/imprisonment for life and even for the offence under Section 471 Indian Penal Code the similar punishment. Apart from that forging and/or manipulating the court record and getting benefit of such forged/manipulated court record was a very serious offence. If the Court record was manipulated and/or forged, it would hamper the administration of justice. Forging/manipulating the Court record and taking the benefit of the same stands on altogether a different footing than forging/manipulating other documents between two individuals. Therefore, the High Court ought to have been more cautious/serious in granting the bail to a person who was alleged to have forged/manipulated the court record and taken the benefit of such manipulated and forged court record more particularly when he had been charge-sheeted having found prima facie case and the charge has been framed.

(ii) Suffice it to say that in the facts and circumstances of the case and looking to the very serious allegations of forging/manipulating court order and having taken advantage of the same, the High Court was not justified in releasing Respondent No. 2 on bail. Merely because the charge-sheet was filed was no ground to release the Accused on bail. The submission on behalf of the Accused that as the record was now in the court's custody there was no chance of tampering was concerned, the allegation against the Respondent Accused were of tampering/forging/manipulating the court record which was in the custody of the court. Seriousness of the offence was one of the relevant considerations while considering the grant of bail, which had not been considered at all by the High Court while releasing Respondent No. 2-Accused on bail.

(iii) The impugned judgment and order passed by the High Court releasing Respondent No. 2-Accused on bail was unsustainable and deserves to be quashed and set aside and was accordingly set aside.

• • •

CHAPTER XV

Union of India Vs Prateek Shukla, 2021

Relevant Sections:

- Narcotic Drugs and Psychotropic Substances Act 1985- Section 8, 9A, 23, 25A and 29

Hon'ble judges: *Dr. D.Y. Chandrachud and M.R. Shah, JJ.*
No. of pdf pages in Original Judgment: 6
Equivalent Citations: AIR2021SC1509, MANU/SC/0176/2021, 2021(2)RCR(Criminal)314

Case note: Narcotics - Bail - Cancellation of - Sections 8, 9A, 23, 25A and 29 of Narcotic Drugs and Psychotropic Substances Act 1985 - Complaint was lodged for offences under Sections 8, 9A, 25A, 23 and 29 of Act - It was alleged that all Accused were members of international drug syndicate and had entered into conspiracy for diversion, illegal storage, sale, purchase and export of controlled substance - Respondent filed bail application which was initially rejected by Additional Sessions Judge - Thereafter, bail application was moved before High Court, which was granted to Respondent - Hence, present appeal - Whether High Court erred in granting to Respondent, who was alleged to be involved in commission of offences punishable under Act, 1985.

Facts: A secret information was received by intelligence officer of the Narcotics Control Bureau that a huge quantity of acetic anhydride had been purchased by a company and that the Company had not submitted its quarterly returns, as required under the Narcotic Drugs and Psychotropic Substances (Regulation of Control Substances) Order 2013. It had been alleged that based on a suspicion of diversion, a team of the NCB proceeded to the Company's registered office. A quantity of acetic anhydride and amphetamine is alleged to have been found in the premises. The Respondent was arrested during the course of the investigation. The lab report allegedly confirmed the presence of acetic anhydride and hydrochloric acid, though the presence of amphetamine has not been specifically recorded and had been sent for further verification. Based on this evidence, a complaint was lodged for offences under Sections 8, 9A,

25A, 23 and 29 of the NDPS Act. It was alleged that all the Accused were members of an international drug syndicate and had entered into a conspiracy for diversion, illegal storage, sale, purchase and export of the controlled substance. The Respondent filed a bail application which was initially rejected by the Additional Sessions Judge. Thereafter, a bail application was moved before the High Court, which was allowed.

Hon'ble Apex court held, while allowing the appeal: (i) Ex facie, there had been no application of mind by the High Court to the rival submissions and, particularly, to the seriousness of the allegations involving an offence punishable under the provisions of the NDPS Act. Merely recording the submissions of the parties does not amount to an indication of a judicial or, for that matter, a judicious application of mind by the Single Judge of the High Court to the basic question as to whether bail should be granted. The provisions of Section 37 of the NDPS Act provide the legal norms which have to be applied in determining whether a case for grant of bail had been made out. There had been a serious infraction by the High Court of its duty to apply the law. The order granting bail was innocent of an awareness of the legal principles involved in determining whether bail should be granted to a person Accused of an offence under the NDPS Act. The contention of the Respondent that he had resigned from the Company must be assessed with reference to the allegations in the criminal complaint which had been filed in the Court of the District and Sessions Judge.

(ii) The contention of the Respondent in the application for bail which was filed before the High Court that he had transferred his shareholding in the Company to director of the company. The director of the prosecution, as the prosecution alleges at this stage, was an Afghan national. The application for bail which had been filed before the High Court as well as the counter affidavit which had been filed in the present proceedings suppress more than what they disclose. Be that as it may, the High Court was clearly not justified in granting bail and the reasons provided by the High Court, did not reflect application of mind to the seriousness of the offence which was involved. Indicating that the Respondent as an educated person with a Bachelor of Technology may not commit any offence was an extraneous circumstance which ought not to have weighed with the High Court in the grant of bail for an offence under the NDPS Act.

∙ ∙ ∙

CHAPTER XVI

Union of India (UOI) Vs. K.A. Najeeb, 2020

Relevant Sections: Narcotic Drugs And Psychotropic Substances Act, 1985 - Section 37; Unlawful Activities (Prevention) Act, 1967 - Section 43-D(5)

Hon'ble judges: N.V. Ramana, Surya Kant and Aniruddha Bose, JJ.

No. of pdf pages in Original Judgment: 8

Equivalent Citations:AIR2021SC712, 2021(2)BLJ142, 2021CriLJ1658, MANU/SC/0046/2021, 2021(2)RCR(Criminal)145

Case note: Criminal - Bail - Grant of - Sections 120-B, 143, 147, 148, 149, 153A, 201, 202, 212, 307, 323, 324, 326, 341 and 427 of Indian Penal Code, 1860, Section 3 of Explosive Substances Act, 1908 and Sections 16, 18, 18-B, 19 and 20 of Unlawful Activities Act, 1967 - FIR was lodged under Sections 143, 147, 148, 120-B, 341, 427, 323, 324, 326, 506(H), 307, 149 of Code and Section 3 of Act - It emerged over course of investigation that attack was part of larger conspiracy involving meticulous pre-planning, numerous failed attempts and use of dangerous weapons - Sections 16, 18, 18-B, 19 and 20 of Act, 1967 was also invoked - Several dozen persons including Respondent were arraigned by police - However, owing to Respondent being untraceable, Respondent was declared absconder and his trial was split up from rest of his co-conspirators - Co-Accused of Respondent were tried and most of them were found guilty by Special Court - Respondent could be arrested and chargesheet was re-filed against him, pursuant to which Respondent was now facing trial - Respondent approached Special Court and High Court for bail which was declined - Respondent again approached High Court questioning Special Court's order denying bail - High Court released Respondent on bail noting that trial was yet to begin though Respondent had been in custody for four years - Hence, present appeal - Whether impugned order of grant of bail warrant any interference.

Facts: An FIR was lodged under Sections 143, 147, 148, 120-B, 341, 427, 323, 324, 326, 506(H), 307, 149 of Indian Penal Code and Section 3 of Explosive Substances Act. It emerged over the course of investigation that the attack was part of a larger conspiracy involving meticulous pre-planning, numerous failed attempts and use of dangerous weapons. Accordingly, several dozen persons including the present Respondent were arraigned by the police. It was alleged that the Respondent was one of the main conspirators and the provisions contained in Sections 153A, 201, 202, 212 of Indian Penal Code, along with Section 16, 18, 18-B, 19 and 20 of the UAPA were also thus invoked against him. However, owing to him being untraceable, the Respondent was declared an absconder and his trial was split up from the rest of his co-conspirators. The co-Accused of the Respondent were tried and most of them were found guilty by the Special Court. The Respondent could be arrested and a chargesheet was re-filed by the National Investigation Agency against him, pursuant to which the Respondent is now facing trial. The Respondent approached the Special Court and the High Court for bail as many as six times. Save for the impugned order, bail was declined to the Respondent, observing that prima facie he had prior knowledge of the offence, had assisted and facilitated the attack, arranged vehicle and SIM cards, himself waited near the place of occurrence, transported the perpetrators, sheltered, and medically assisted them afterwards. The Courts were, therefore, of the view that the bar against grant of bail under Section 43-D(5) of the UAPA was attracted. The Respondent again approached the High Court questioning the Special Court's order denying bail. The High Court through the impugned order, released the Respondent on bail noting that the trial was yet to begin though the Respondent had been in custody for four years.

Hon'ble Apex court held, while dismissing the appeal: (i) It was a fact that the High Court in the instant case had not determined the likelihood of the Respondent being guilty or not, or whether rigours of Section 43-D(5) of UAPA are alien to him. The High Court instead appears to have exercised its power to grant bail owing to the long period of incarceration and the unlikelihood of the trial being completed anytime in the near future. The reasons assigned by the High Court were apparently traceable back to Article 21 of Constitution, of course without addressing the statutory embargo created by Section 43-D(5) of UAPA.

(ii) Not only had the Respondent been in jail for much more than five years, but there were several witnesses left to be examined. Charges had been framed. Still further, two opportunities were given to the Appellant who had shown no inclination to screen its endless list of witnesses. It also deserves mention that of the thirteen co-Accused who had been convicted, none had been given a sentence of more than eight years rigorous imprisonment. It could therefore be legitimately expected that if found guilty, the Respondent too would receive a sentence within the same ballpark. Given that two-third of such incarceration was already complete, it appears that the Respondent had already paid heavily for his acts of fleeing from justice.

(iii) The charges levelled against the Respondent were grave and a serious threat to societal harmony. Had it been a case at the threshold, this court would have outrightly turned down the Respondent's prayer. However, keeping in mind the length of the period spent by him in custody and the unlikelihood of the trial being completed anytime soon, the High Court appears to have been left with no other option except to grant bail. An attempt had been made to strike a balance between the Appellant's right to lead evidence of its choice and establish the charges beyond any doubt and simultaneously the Respondent's rights guaranteed under Part III of our Constitution have been well protected.

Ratio Decidendi:

The presence of statutory restrictions like Section 43-D(5) of UAPA per-se does not oust the ability of Constitutional Courts to grant bail on grounds of violation of Part III of the Constitution.

• • •

CHAPTER XVII

Naresh Kumar Mangla Vs. Anita Agarwal and Ors., 2020

Relevant Sections:

- IPC- Section34,149,304B,313,323,468,471,498A,506
- CRPC-Section 46(1), 154, 438, 439

Hon'ble judges: Dr. D.Y. Chandrachud, Indu Malhotra and Indira Banerjee, JJ.

No. of pdf pages in Original Judgment: 20

Equivalent Citations: AIR2021SC277, 2020(12)ADJ622, 2021(1)Crimes105(SC), I(2021)DMC62SC, 2021(1)MLJ(Crl)170, 2021 (1) MWN (CR.) 109, MANU/SC/0951/2020, 2021(1)N.C.C.128, 2021(1)UC231

Case note: Criminal - Anticipatory bail - Cancellation of - Sections 304-B, 313, 323, 498-A and 506 of Indian Penal Code, 1860 and Sections 3 and 4 of Dowry Prohibition Act, 1961 - Applications for anticipatory bail filed by four out of five persons who had been named as Accused in case registered under Sections 498A, 304-B, 323, 506 and 313 of Code and Sections 3/4 of Act - Husband of deceased was in custody - Single Judge of High Court allowed applications and granted them anticipatory bail - Hence, present appeal - Whether High Court erred in granting anticipatory bail to accused persons.

Facts: FIR was registered against accused persons for offence under Sections 498A, 304-B, 323, 506 and 313 of the Indian Penal Code and Sections 3/4 of the Dowry Prohibition Act, 1961. The Sessions Judge noted that besides naming the Accused specifically, there were also allegations against the four Respondents in the FIR of torturing the deceased and of making demands for dowry. Non-bailable warrants were issued against the four Accused. Applications for anticipatory bail were filed on their behalf before the High Court. A Single Judge of the High Court allowed the applications and granted them anticipatory bail.

Hon'ble Apex court held, while allowing the appeal: (i) The judgment of the Single Judge of the High Court was unsustainable. The FIR contains a recital of allegations bearing on the role of the Accused in demanding dowry, of the prior incidents of assault and the payment of moneys by cheque to the in-laws of the deceased. The FIR had referred to the telephone calls which were received both from the father-in-law of the deceased on the morning and from the deceased on two occasions on the same day-a few hours before her body was found. The grant of anticipatory bail in such a serious offence would operate to obstruct the investigation. The FIR by a father who had suffered the death of his daughter in these circumstances could not be regarded as engineered to falsely implicate the spouse of the deceased and his family.

(ii) It was necessary to entrust a further investigation of the case to the CBI in exercise of the powers of this Court under Article 142 of the Constitution. The conduct of the investigating authorities from the stage of arriving at the scene of occurrence to the filing of the charge-sheet did not inspire confidence in the robustness of the process. A perusal of the charge-sheet evinces a perfunctory rendition of the investigating authorities duty by a bare reference to the facts and the presumption under Section 304B of the IPC (Indian Penal Code) when the death occurs within seven years of the marriage. The stance taken by the Deputy Superintendent of Police in the Counter Affidavit, filed a few days after forwarding the charge-sheet, travels beyond the scope of the investigation recorded in the charge-sheet with respect to the veracity of the suicide note, medical examination of injuries and the past miscarriages of the deceased. Critical facts of the money trail between the deceased, her father (the informant), and the Accused and the call history of A2, the informant and the deceased were unexplored. No attempt at custodial interrogation of the applicants was made between the issuance of non-bailable warrants and interim protection from arrest by the High Court granted. Upon questioning during the hearing, the Counsel for the State answered that no investigation on the allegation of murder had been conducted. It would indeed be a travesty if this Court were to ignore the glaring deficiencies in the investigation conducted so far, irrespective of the stage of the proceedings or the nature of the question before this Court. The status of the Accused as propertied and wealthy persons of influence in Agra and the conduct of the investigation thus far diminishes this Court's faith in directing a further investigation by the same authorities. The cause of justice would not be served if the Court were to confine the scope of its examination to the wisdom of granting anticipatory bail and ignore the possibility of a trial being concluded on the basis of a deficient investigation at best or a biased one at worst.

∙ ∙ ∙

CHAPTER XVIII

Venkatesan Balasubramaniyan and Ors.Vs. The Intelligence Officer, D.R.I. Bangalore, 2020

Relevant Sections: CRPC- Section 439,167(2)
   Hon'ble judges: Ashok Bhushan, R. Subhash Reddy and M.R. Shah, JJ.
   No. of pdf pages in Original Judgment: 8
   Equivalent Citations:2021(218)AIC254, AIR2021SC335, 2020(4)Crimes415(SC), 2021CriLJ978, 2020(374)ELT845(S.C.), 2020(6)JKJ70[SC], 2020 (6) KHC 468, MANU/SC/0878/2020, 2021(1)RLW321(SC)

Case note: Criminal - Cancellation of Bail - Section 439(2) of the Code of Criminal Procedure, 1973 (CrPC) - Correctness thereof - Appellants arrested for carrying packets of Narcotic Drugs - Granted Default Bail on the expiry of 180 days under Section 167(2), CrPC - Appellants served notice for their custody and to appear before Court where transit had originated - DRI/ Respondent applied for cancellation of Bail - High Court vide impugned judgment cancelled Bail granted - Hence, the present appeal - Whether statutory bail granted in default liable to be rejected?

Facts: High Court vide impugned judgment allowed petition filed by Respondent seeking cancellation of bail granted to the Appellants. Appellants were found to be carrying packets of Narcotic drug to be delivered at a designated place. Appellants were arrested and crime report was prepared for commission of offence under Sections 22, 28 and 29 of NDPS Act. On the expiry of 180 days, Appellants filed bail application, which was granted under Section 167(2) Code of Criminal Procedure. Fact about other complaints not disclosed. Custody accordingly was sought. High Court on Respondent's application cancelled the bail granted. Hence, the present appeal.

Hon'ble Apex court held, while dismissing the appeal: i. It was not even submitted that Omerga Court where common complaint has been filed against the Accused had no jurisdiction to inquire and try the offence. It was due to some miscommunication that at the time when Court passed the order on 12.07.2018, the factum of filing of combined complaint dated 06.07.2018 was not brought into the notice of Special Court, Hyderabad. Although, letter of the same date 12.07.2018 was received by Special Court,

Hyderabad from Special Court, Omerga praying for custody of the Appellants, which custody was also granted by the Special Court, Hyderabad on the next day. All these facts were brought before the High Court in application filed under Section 439(2) Code of Criminal Procedure and the High Court has rightly cancelled the bail order dated 12.07.2018.

ii. There is ample material in the complaint that the transportation of narcotic substance started from Omerga, Maharashtra and was being allegedly to be taken to Chennai and intercepted at Hyderabad. The combined complaint having been filed on 06.07.2018, i.e., well within 180 days, the High Court did not commit any error in cancelling the default bail granted to the Appellants on 12.07.2018.

iii. No ground for interfering with the impugned judgment/order of the High Court. All the appeals are dismissed subject to liberty granted to the Appellants.

• • •

CHAPTER XIX

R. DAMODARAN Vs. THE STATE REPRESENTED BY THE INSPECTOR OF POLICE, 2021

Relevant Sections:

- CRPC-174,313
- IPC-302,304

Hon'ble judges: Ashok Bhushan and Ajay Rastogi, JJ.
No. of pdf pages in Original Judgment: 6
Equivalent Citations: AIR2021SC1173, 2021CriLJ1458, MANU/SC/0109/2021, 2021(2)RCR(Criminal)199

Case note: Criminal - Murder - Conviction - Circumstantial Evidence- Section 302 of the Indian Penal Code, 1860 (IPC) -Appellant accused of murdering his own wife - Wife after being hit by Appellant taken to hospital citing her to have suffered cardiac arrest - Autopsy confirmed death caused due to shock and haemorrhage - Appellant prosecuted and held guilty - Hence, the present appeal - Whether Appellant rightly convicted for murdering his wife?

Facts: The Accused Appellant was convicted for offence under Section 302 of the Indian Penal Code, 1860 (IPC) for murdering his own wife while she was at the advanced stage of her pregnancy. High Court vide judgment impugned confirmed the finding of Trial Court. As alleged, Appellant used to frequently change his rented accommodation and on each change used to make deceased fetch money from her father. He was alleged of beating and quarrelling deceased under the influence of liquor and on the fateful night he picked up a log from the house and beaten deceased that caused internal injury in her stomach and murdered her. Appellant pleaded that death occurred due to cardiac arrest.

Hon'ble Apex court held, while dismissing the appeal: It was the Appellant himself who took her to the hospital and made a false statement that she suffered a cardiac arrest but after the autopsy was conducted on the body of the deceased, it was opined that she died out of shock and haemorrhage due to thoracic injuries. In addition to other circumstances, the prosecution was able to establish that it was none other than the

Appellant who had committed the crime and he wanted to show his innocence by taking the deceased to the hospital and made a false statement that she suffered a cardiac arrest which on receipt of the post-mortem certificate, was found to be false where it was established that the death was caused by homicidal violence.

The prosecution established chain of events that leave no matter of doubt that it is none other than the Appellant who had committed the crime of murdering his own wife.

The present case squarely rests on circumstantial evidence where the death has been caused by homicidal violence and the Appellant who had himself taken the deceased to the hospital and made a false statement to the Doctor that she had suffered a cardiac arrest which was found to be false after the postmortem report was received and the nature of injuries which were attributed on the body of the deceased of which a reference has been made clearly establish that it is the case where none other than the Accused Appellant has committed a commission of crime with intention to commit the murder of his own wife who was at the advanced stage of pregnancy.

No substance in the appeal and is accordingly dismissed.

Appellant's bail bonds stand cancelled. The Appellant is directed to surrender within four weeks from today and undergo the remaining part of sentence.

Ratio Decidendi:

Circumstances from which the conclusion of guilt is to be drawn should be fully proved and conclusive in nature.

• • •

CHAPTER XX

20. Mauji Ram Vs. State of Uttar Pradesh and Ors, 2019

Relevant Sections:

- CRPC- Section 439

Hon'ble judges: Abhay Manohar Sapre and Indu Malhotra, JJ
No. of pdf pages in Original Judgment: 5
Equivalent Citations: 2019(203)AIC187, AIR2019SC4430, 2019ALLMR(Cri)3932, 2019 (109) ACC 630, 2019(3)ACR2811, 2020(3) ALJ 220, 2019(3)Crimes263(SC), 2019(5)JKJ429[SC], 2020(1)JCC97, MANU/SC/0991/2019, 2019(3)RCR(Criminal)969, 2019(10)SCALE64, (2019)8SCC17, 2019(2)UC1361

Case note: Criminal - Grant of bail - Challenge thereto - Section 302 Indian Penal Code, 1860 (IPC) - Present appeals were directed against orders of High Court granting bail to Respondents - Whether the High Court was justified in granting bail to the Respondents (Accused)

Facts: Respondents (Accused persons) after they were apprehended applied for grant of bail before the Sessions Court in the aforementioned trial. The Sessions Judge by order rejected the bail applications of the Respondents. Respondents felt aggrieved by the rejection of their bail applications and filed the bail applications under Section 439 of the Criminal Procedure Code, 1973 (CrPC) in the High Court of. By impugned orders, the High Court allowed the bail applications and accordingly directed release of the Respondents on bail on their furnishing security and bail bonds to the satisfaction of the Sessions Judge. It is against these orders of the High Court, the father of the deceased has felt aggrieved and filed these appeals questioning the legality and correctness of the impugned orders.

Hon'ble Apex court held, while allowing the appeal: 1. High Court committed jurisdictional error in passing the impugned order because while passing the impugned order, the High Court did not assign any reason whatsoever as to on what grounds, even though of a prima facie nature, it considered just and proper to grant bail to the Respondents.

2. Time and again this Court has emphasized the need for assigning the reasons while granting bail. Though it may not be necessary to give categorical finding while granting or rejecting the bail for want of full evidence adduced by the prosecution as also by the defence at that stage yet it must appear from a perusal of the order that the Court has applied its mind to the relevant facts in the light of the material filed by the prosecution at the time of consideration of bail application. It is unfortunate that neither the law laid down by this Court, nor the material filed by the prosecution was taken note of by the High Court while considering the grant of bail to the Respondents.

3. In view the antecedents of the Accused persons which are brought on record by the State in their counter affidavit and further keeping in view the manner in which the offence under Section 302 of IPC was committed, present Court prima facie of the view that, this is not a fit case for grant of bail to the Accused persons (Respondent No. 2 herein in all the appeals). These factors were relevant while considering the bail application and, in our view, they were not taken into consideration.

4. The Sessions Judge was, therefore, right in rejecting the bail applications filed by the Respondents.

5. Impugned orders are set aside. The bail applications filed by the Respondents (Accused persons) are dismissed. Appeal allowed.

6. As a consequence thereof, the Respondents (Accused persons) in all the appeals are directed to surrender in the concerned Sessions Court for being taken into custody as under trial.

• • •

Videos & Tv Shows On Law & Exim

List of some important videos & TV shows on Law & EXIM by Adv. Jayprakash Somani on his YouTube Channel 'Jayprakash Somani EXIM & Legal'

Legal Videos: Hindi -English

1) SLP in Supreme Court / Special Leave Petitions in the Supreme Court of India
2) Transfer of Civil & Criminal Cases by the Supreme Court of India / Transfer of Matrimonial Cases
3) Appellate Jurisdiction of the Supreme Court of India
4) Jurisdictions of the Supreme Court of India
5) Public Interest Litigation in the Supreme Court of India / PIL in Supreme Court
6) Article 32 Writ Petitions in the Supreme Court of India
7) Bail Matters Top 10 Supreme Court Cases
8) FIR Quashing in High Court & Supreme Court
9) Bail & Anticipatory Bail Matters in Supreme Court
10) Insolvency & Bankruptcy Matters in the Supreme Court
11) Insolvency & Bankruptcy Code 2016 Part 1
12) Insolvency & Bankruptcy Code 2016 Part 2
13) Insolvency & Bankruptcy Code 2016 Part 3
14) Corporate Liquidation Process
15) Supreme Court Rules & Procedures Webinar of 2.5 hour on Zoom
16) RDDBFI Act, 1993 (Introduction)
17) The Indian Contact Act 1872
18) Negotiable Instruments Act (Introduction)
19) How to avoid matrimonial disputes & some more videos
20) SEBI Matters in the Supreme Court
21) Matrimonial Matters: Supreme Court's 20 Case Laws
22) Consumer Matters Supreme Court's 20 Case Laws
23) Service Matters Supreme Court's 20 Case Laws
24) How to Search Lawyer for Your Matter
25) Property Matters Supreme Court's 20 Case Laws
26) Bail Matters: Supreme Court's 20 Case Laws
27) Supreme Court / High Court Vacation Benches

28) 69000 Teacher's Recruitment Matters of UP Government in the Supreme Court
29) Contempt of Court Matters in the Supreme Court
30) Advocate Act's Matters in the Supreme Court
31) Business Law Matters in the Supreme Court
32) Banking Matters in the Supreme Court
33) Labour Law Matters in the Supreme Court
34) Arbitration Matters in the Supreme Court
35) Careers in Law -Zoom Webinar by Adv. Jayprakash Somani
36) Civil Matters in the Supreme Court
37) Consumer Protection Act | Consumer Matters in the Supreme Court
38) Corporate Matters in the Supreme Court
39) Criminal Matters in the Supreme Court
40) Role of Respondent in the Supreme Court of India
41) Motor Vehicle Accident Matters in Supreme Court with case laws
42) Article 131 Original Suits in Supreme Court
43) PIL in Supreme Court/ Public Interest Litigations in the Supreme Court of India'
44) CAB Citizenship Amendment Bill is not Unconstitutional
45) Supreme Court of India Cases & Process – Marathi
46) Legal Services Export / Export of Legal Services
47) Transfer of Matrimonial Cases by the Supreme Court of India
48) Public Interest Litigation PIL
49) The Specific Relief Act (Introduction)
50) Corporate Insolvency Resolution Process CIRP
51) ABMM's Career 5 - Careers in Law
52) Transfer of cases by Supreme Court
53) Writ Petitions in High Court & Supreme Court of India
54) Supreme Court Jurisdictions - Appeals, SLP, Writ Petitions, Transfer, Original, Review, Curative
55) LEGAL INDIA TV Show: Cases Handled in Supreme Court
56) Corporate Liquidation Process
57) Legal Services Export / Export of Legal Services

EXIM Videos: Hindi -English
1) Yes, I can do Import Export Business Easily! 36 points excellent video in Hindi
2) Yes, I can do Import Export Business Easily! 36 points excellent video in English

VIDEOS & TV SHOWS ON LAW & EXIM

3) Import Export Business – Hindi video
4) Import Export Business - English video
5) Export Import Marathi TV Interview
6) Scope for Commerce Students in International Business- TV Show
7) Scope for Management Student in International Business- TV Show
8) Scope for Engineering Students in International Business – TV Show
9) Women in International Business- TV Show
10) How to do Import Export Business Successfully!'
11) Where one can get full information on Import Export Business?
12) What to do import & export?
13) Import Export Workshop/ Training/Course/ Diploma
14) How to Start Import Export Business & How to grow it. Live Webinar
15) Success Stories & Failure Stories in Import & Export Business
16) For MSME Scope in Export & Import...
17) Exports In Agri. & Food Products – English & some more videos
18) Exports to Dubai, Aabudhabii. e. UAE
19) Jewellery Exports from India
20) How to attend EXIM workshop to become excellent Exporter
21) Import Export Best Training Course – Online & Offline
22) Agri Product Export
23) Scope for Woman in International Business
24) Management Graduates Scope in International Business
25) Pharma Product's Export
26) Best Import Export Course | Practical Training | Aaronica Global Exim
27) Import Export Business for Commerce Graduates
28) How Do I Get Export Orders? Finding International Buyers
29) What Is APEDA In Import Export Business?
30) Which Is The Best Product To Export From India?
31) EXIM Remark by Manoj Kumar Faridabad
32) EXIM Remarks by Mahesh Telangana
33) What Licenses I Need To Start Import/ Export?
34) How Can I Increase My Import Export Business?
35) Which Is Best B2B Website For Import/Export Business?
36) Export Import Management with Global Marketing
37) How to Start Export Import Business | 51 Points Video
38) Scope for Commerce & Other Graduates in International Business

VIDEOS & TV SHOWS ON LAW & EXIM

39) BE A SUCCESSFUL EXPORTER FOR OUR NATION - Marathi video
40) Export of Textile, Cotton, Agri., Food, & other products & services
41) Exports from MP, CG, MH, GJ & CA in Fresh Fruits & Vegetables
42) Exports in Agri. & Food Products- Hindi
43) Start your Online/E-Commerce Business
44) How to Start Export Import Business & Grow it
45) Exports in Textile & Other Products
46) Start and grow EXIM business - Live English Webinar
47) 'Import Export Business!' Why, Who, What & How can one do it easily!!
48) Live: Export of Product & Services During & After Lock Down Period
49) Frauds in Import Export Business
50) Import Export for Business Man
51) Import & Export for Women
51) Import & Export for Graduate & Post - Graduate Students
52) Agriculture Exports from India
53) Digital Marketing Setup - Marathi
54) 2nd Secret of Successful Businessman
55) Digital Marketing Set up
56) Legal Services Export / Export of Legal Services
57) Export & Import with UAE
58) Service Exports / Exports by Service Providers
59) Import Export Workshop/ Training/Course/ Diploma
60) Exports & Imports with USA
61) Selection on Product for Export
62) Top Products Exported from India
63) What to do import & export?
64) ABMM Career 2 - 'Careers in Business & Industries
65) How to do Import Export Business Successfully!'
66) 5 Secrets of Successful Businessman
67) Export from MP, Chhattisgarh & Vidarbha Nagpur
68) EXIM Hindi - Textile & Apparel Export
69) EXIM Hindi - Export Import Practical Training In Delhi, Kolkata, Mumbai and Pune
70) Import Export Business
71) Import Export Business Hindi
72) Import Export Business English video

73) Import Export Business Marathi

74) Women in International Business by Exim Guru Adv. Jayprakash Somani

75) Opportunities in Foreign Trade- Adv. Jayprakash Somani's special interview

∙ ∙ ∙

List Of Books

List of Adv. Jayprakash Somani's Books
1. Supreme Court of India's Leading Case Laws on 'Insolvency & Bankruptcy Code 2016'
2. Bail Matters – Supreme Court's Latest Leading Case Laws
3. Arbitration Matters- Supreme Court's Latest Leading Case Laws
4. Property Matters - Supreme Court's Latest Leading Case Laws
5. Matrimonial Matters- Supreme Court's Latest Leading Case Laws
6. Election Matters- Supreme Court's Latest Leading Case Laws
7. SEBI Matters- Supreme Court's Latest Leading Case Laws
8. Banking Matters- Supreme Court's Latest Leading Case Laws
9. Service Matters- Supreme Court's Latest Leading Case Laws
10. Contempt of Court Matters- Supreme Court's Latest Leading Case Laws
11. Consumer Protection Matters- Supreme Court's Latest Leading Case Laws
12. Corporate Law- Supreme Court's Latest Leading Case Laws
13. Completion Act - Supreme Court's Latest Leading Case Laws

• • •

These Books are available online at

1. **Notion Press:**https://notionpress.com/author/jayprakash_somani
2. **Amazon:**https://www.amazon.in/s?k=jayprakash+somani
3. **Flipkart:**https://www.flipkart.com/search?q=Jayprakash%20Somani

• • •

www.ingramcontent.com/pod-product-compliance
Lightning Source LLC
Chambersburg PA
CBHW070820220526
45466CB00002B/726